DR. NELSON K. WILLIAMS

SITTING ON THE PORCH

Cover Design: Mrs. Eboneé Pemberton

Cover Design Concept: Dr. Nelson Williams

Edited by: Mrs. Lillian Williams

Book Layout Design Editor: Ms. Oana Rafaila

Mrs. Mamie Willams
(Grandma)

Table of Contents

Introduction

Growing up, one of my most favorite places was the porch. I remember spending time with my grandmother, Mrs. Mamie Williams, sitting on the porch. In the morning, when the birds were just waking and singing, the porch beckoned us to bask in its comfort, while cool breezes flowed through the nearby trees and meadows. This beckoning was normally accompanied by a hot cup of coffee, a hot chocolate, or a cold glass of tea in the heat of the day. As I fondly reminisce, time passed slowly on the porch, yet I could spend the whole day there. It allowed me to spend time with family and friends in the early light of day or evening sunset, as the light from the moon danced over the trees. So many precious life-changing memories came from time spent on the porch. Overall, the porch had a way of impacting our day and ultimately became a part of shaping how we valued life.

Generally, a porch is a covered area that is attached to the entrance of a home. A porch typically has open sides and offers an easy transition between the indoors and outdoors. Sitting on the porch requires a comfortable rocking chair or slightly squeaky porch swing with a table set to provide the right amount of casual and cozy amenities, which creates the perfect atmosphere. I sincerely think that all homes should have porches or at least a balcony or deck. For one thing, they have many practical uses: provide shade from the smoldering heat of the summer, help keep homes cool during warm days, and during the winter, the porch provides a warming element from the sun. Additionally, porches serve as a barrier to the snow from the door, providing a transition space, so you don't feel besieged by the often harsh winter weather.

For decades and in many cultures, the front porch has served as a place where families have sat and relaxed after a meal while listening to music, having casual conversation, debating sports, or hearing the voices of playing children. The porch also served as a convenient space for couriers to leave packages and guests to enter your space. Plus, it gave a home some serious curb appeal. The porch is a place where stars were counted in the sky, dates kissed good night while dad or mom flickered the lights saying, "time's up," and a place where many other great memories were born. Grandpas and grandmas have shared many stories on front porches. In my younger days, it was even where garden peas were shelled during a thought-provoking conversation, and tea was sipped. When the temperature was just right, it was an ideal spot to kick back and relax.

Andrew Jackson Downing popularized the front porch as an iconic feature in American homes. Downing was a landscape architect who lived in the early 1800s. He popularized the front porch in his writings and designs, as a way to link homes and their occupants with nature. Interestingly, Downing believed that the architecture of a home could affect the morals of its residents. He believed it was critical to build homes that were beautiful, functional, and integrated with their natural surroundings (richlyrooted.com). Large or small, many of our modern-day homes lack the unassuming graciousness of a front porch. On houses that do have porches, you don't see people using them as much as we did back in the day. Remember the *Andy Griffith Show* with characters: Andy, Aunt B, Barney, Opie, and Helen in the small town of Mayberry? I still remember those episodes from times past. In the evenings, the town residents would sit out on the porch, exchange pleasantries, and sometimes sing together, just being friendly and neighborly. In this century, we've nearly lost that sense of community in the busyness of life: the constant activities of the kids, the heavy demands of work, and electronic devices that pull us inside and away from others. Surprisingly, amid the global pandemic, front porches, balconies, and patios everywhere were being used again. People were simply elated to get out of the house. We were fellowshipping, playing instruments, and singing songs in the open air of the front porch again. More importantly, the porch, on many occasions, served as a place of mental and spiritual healing.

Significance of the Porch in the Holy Bible

Porches played significant roles in the Bible. Solomon's Porch was the name of two porches associated with the temple in Jerusalem. In the Holy Bible, Solomon's Porch was a grand covered walkway with massive columns that was named for King Solomon, who built the First Temple of the Jews, a magnificent holy structure in ancient Jerusalem. This covered area became a significant gathering place for intellectual discourse and debate. It was also a place where Jesus taught, shared, healed, and visited with people (JOHN 10) and where his disciples continued Jesus' ministry (ACTS 3, 5).

The original temple constructed by King Solomon is described in 1 Kings, "As for the house which King Solomon built for the LORD, its length was sixty cubits [90 feet] and its width twenty cubits [30 feet] and its height thirty cubits [45 feet]. The porch in front of the nave of the house was twenty cubits [30 feet] in length, corresponding to the width of the house, and its depth along the front of the house was ten cubits [15 feet]" (1 KINGS 6:2-3).

The Jewish historian, Josephus, describes Solomon's Porch this way, "There was a porch without the temple, overlooking a deep valley, supported by walls of four hundred cubits, made of four square stones, very white; the length of each stone was twenty cubits, and the breadth six; the work of king Solomon, who first founded the whole temple" (ANTIQUITIES L. 20. C. 8. SECT. 7).

One winter, at the Festival of Dedication (or Hanukkah), Jesus was in Jerusalem, and John describes Him as "in the temple courts walking in Solomon's Colonnade" (JOHN 10:23). The King James Version (KJV) says, "Solomon's Porch." In ACTS 5:12, Solomon's Porch was the gathering place for believers in Jerusalem before the Diaspora, the settling of scattered colonies of Jews outside Palestine after the Babylonian exile. Earlier, in ACTS 3:11, Peter and John had healed a lame man at Solomon's Porch and preached to a large crowd that had gathered there. It was Church Service on the porch!

ACTS 3:1 Now Peter and John went up together to the temple at the hour of prayer, the ninth hour. 2 And a certain man lame from his mother's womb was carried, whom they laid daily at the gate of the temple, which is called Beautiful, to ask alms from those who entered the temple; 3 who, seeing Peter and John about to go into the temple, asked for alms. 4 And fixing his eyes on him, with John, Peter said, "Look at us." 5 So he gave them his attention, expecting to receive something from them. 6 Then Peter said, "Silver and gold I do not have, but what I do have I give you: In the name of Jesus Christ of Nazareth, rise up and walk." 7 And he took him by the right hand and lifted him up, and immediately his feet and ankle bones received strength.

8   So he, leaping up, stood and walked and entered the temple with them—walking, leaping, and praising God.   9   And all the people saw him walking and praising God.   10   Then they knew that it was he who sat begging alms at the Beautiful Gate of the temple; and they were filled with wonder and amazement at what had happened to him. 11   Now as the lame man who was healed held on to Peter and John, all the people ran together to them in the porch which is called Solomon's, greatly amazed.

OBSERVATIONS
FROM
THE PORCH

———————

I invite you to sit on the porch with me to glean divine wisdom and cherish the moments.

History Lessons

The porch was a place of learning history. My grandmother would share valuable information about the family when we sat on the porch, especially memories of Papa, my grandfather, who had passed away when I was only a toddler. Through my grandmother's storytelling, I was given a glimpse of the life of my Papa and his legacy for our family. Grandmother would also use that time on the porch to share her faith and teach us Bible stories and important scriptures that we should commit to memory. Her teachings from the Bible strengthened us and are still engrafted in our hearts and have shaped who we are today. It's true that most of the well-known people of the Bible were grandparents. Many played a key role in history, and each had something to teach parents today. Throughout scripture, you find that grandparents, often referred to as elders, forefathers, or ancestors, are crucial to God's plan of salvation for the whole world. Grandparents have the responsibility of ensuring that the faith in the Gospel of Jesus Christ is passed down from generation to generation. Grandmother would often emphasize in her unique way that if you are a doer of the word of God and not a hearer only, you reap the wonderful benefits that come with it.

2 TIMOTHY 1:5   When I call to remembrance the genuine faith that is in you, which dwelt first in your grandmother Lois and your mother Eunice, and I am persuaded is in you also.

ACTS 5:12   And through the hands of the apostles many signs and wonders were done among the people. And they were all with one accord in Solomon's Porch. 13   Yet none of the rest dared join them, but the people esteemed them highly.

14   And believers were increasingly added to the Lord, multitudes of both men and women, 15 so that they brought the sick out into the streets and laid them on beds and couches, that at least the shadow of Peter passing by might fall on some of them. 16 Also a multitude gathered from the surrounding cities to Jerusalem, bringing sick people and those who were tormented by unclean spirits, and they were all healed.

ISAIAH 55:10   "For as the rain comes down, and the snow from heaven, and do not return there, but water the earth, and make it bring forth and bud, that it may give seed to the sower and bread to the eater, 11 So shall My word be that goes forth from My mouth; It shall not return to Me void, but it shall accomplish what I please, and it shall prosper in the thing for which I sent it.

A Place of Rest

After a long day or playing in the yard as a boy, the porch was a place of rest. When I would run around barefooted in the front yard of my grandmother's house, shaded by a big tree, the porch was almost never empty. Sitting in the swing or rocking chair just soaking in the sunset, the porch was a great place for decompressing as the day came to a close. The porch, in essence, was an outdoor living room, where the family could retire after the activities of a long day. When we worked on the farm, front-porch sitting was a ritual that no one even talked about. It was just what people did—after lunch, bellies full, recovering before climbing back on the tractor or in the bed of the pickup truck to head back out to the tobacco fields. Of course, after lunch and after supper, we sat sedately on that great, big porch. However, during the daytime it was extremely active, voices echoing in the fields or in the pastures as we checked on the cattle, or later in the season, in the tobacco stripping room tucked inside the big barn. It was hard work, but those were the days! Finally, after a long day of work, the porch was a place of rest, as it remains today.

ISAIAH 40:29   He gives power to the weak,
And to those who have no might He increases strength.
30   Even the youths shall faint and be weary,
And the young men shall utterly fall,
31   But those who wait on the Lord
Shall renew their strength;
They shall mount up with wings like eagles,
They shall run and not be weary,
They shall walk and not faint.

MATTHEW 11:28   Come to Me, all you who labor and are heavy laden, and I will give you rest.   29   Take My yoke upon you and learn from Me, for I am gentle and lowly in heart, and you will find rest for your souls. 30 For My yoke is easy and My burden is light."

HEBREWS 4:1 Therefore, since a promise remains of entering His rest, let us fear lest any of you seem to have come short of it. 2 For indeed the gospel was preached to us as well as to them; but the word which they heard did not profit them, not being mixed with faith in those who heard it. 3 For we who have believed do enter that rest, as He has said:
"So I swore in My wrath,
'They shall not enter My rest,'"
although the works were finished from the foundation of the world.

HEBREWS 4:9 There remains therefore a rest for the people of God. 10 For he who has entered His rest has himself also ceased from his works as God did from His. 11 Let us therefore be diligent to enter that rest, lest anyone fall according to the same example of disobedience.

A Getaway

The porch became a place to get away from the hustle and bustle in the house. There is something that feels profoundly right about being on a front porch. It's kind of like the beach—it feels perfect, like it's where you belong, and you neither need nor want to leave. It has all the advantages of being in your own space, yet at the same time all the advantages of being out in the world enjoying the beauty of God's handiwork. People like the idea of porch sitting, but we don't do it as much as we should anymore. Our days are too crowded for us to think of "sitting a spell" and basically taking time out from the hustle and bustle. When we do have pauses in our day, we're prone to reading the newspaper, a book, or checking apps and social media.

MARK 6:31   And He said to them, "Come aside by yourselves to a deserted place and rest a while." For there were many coming and going, and they did not even have time to eat.   32   So they departed to a deserted place in the boat by themselves.

EPHESIANS 5:15   See then that you walk circumspectly, not as fools but as wise,   16   redeeming the time, because the days are evil.   17   Therefore do not be unwise, but understand what the will of the Lord is.

PSALM 55:6 So I said, "Oh, that I had wings like a dove!
I would fly away and be at rest.
7   Indeed, I would wander far off,
And remain in the wilderness. Selah
8   I would hasten my escape
From the windy storm and tempest."

A Greeting Place

The porch is frequently a greeting place for guests and a place to entertain guests. On a nice day, the guests may not have made it inside the house. The porch would suffice. Many times, the porch creates a perfect atmosphere that is warm and welcoming. There is power on the porch to connect us to others. We only have to learn to use it again. The porch is also a place where neighbors left things like borrowed tools, missed deliveries, an extra bag of vegetables, mail, and invitations. Sometimes even home cooked pies or cakes would appear on the porch from neighbors or relatives. This was common in the country, down south in North Carolina, where I was raised. My grandmother's porch was symbolic of a friendly and peaceful place.

MATTHEW 10:12   And when you go into a household, greet it.   13   If the household is worthy, let your peace come upon it. But if it is not worthy, let your peace return to you.   14   And whoever will not receive you nor hear your words, when you depart from that house or city, shake off the dust from your feet.

ROMANS 12:13   Contribute to the needs of the saints and seek to show hospitality.

ISAIAH 41:10   Fear not, for I am with you; be not dismayed, for I am your God; I will strengthen you, I will help you, I will uphold you with my righteous right hand.

PHILIPPIANS 2:3   Let nothing be done through selfish ambition or conceit, but in lowliness of mind let each esteem others better than himself.

A Place to Dine

We would get together after school or work on nice autumn evenings, pour ourselves glasses of tea and chat or read, as we watched people drive or walk by the porch. My mother made the best hush puppies to go with our tea! It's still one of my favorites... deep-fried round ball made from cornmeal-based batter, piping hot with a glass of cool, sweet tea. The porch was also a favorite place for my cousin and I to eat watermelon or a nice dessert while conversing about all sorts of things concerning our lives, future plans, and ideas. Everyone looked forward to gathering on grandmother's porch for dinner and to wind down after a long day. The meal was always amazing, but it seemed better to eat on the porch while looking over the wooded areas on our land with rows of fresh vegetables, fruit and pecan trees, and vast farmland. Sometimes we had so many on the porch for dinner that we had to push two or three tables together and/or bring out extra chairs to accommodate family, friends, and neighbors. It was just great to be on the porch for dinner, even if we sat on the edge of the porch with our legs dangling off. It was all about being together in one place, dining together on the porch.

ACTS 2:46　So continuing daily with one accord in the temple, and breaking bread from house to house, they ate their food with gladness and simplicity of heart, 47　praising God and having favor with all the people. And the Lord added to the church daily those who were being saved.

JOHN 21:9　Then, as soon as they had come to land, they saw a fire of coals there, and fish laid on it, and bread. 10　Jesus said to them, "Bring some of the fish which you have just caught." 11　Simon Peter went up and dragged the net to land, full of large fish, one hundred and fifty-three; and although there were so many, the net was not broken. 12 Jesus said to them, "Come and eat breakfast." Yet none of the disciples dared ask Him, "Who are You?"—knowing that it was the Lord. 13 Jesus then came and took the bread and gave it to them, and likewise the fish. 14 This is now the third time Jesus showed Himself to His disciples after He was raised from the dead. 15 So when they had eaten breakfast, Jesus said to Simon Peter, "Simon, son of Jonah, do you love Me more than these?"

He said to Him, "Yes, Lord; You know that I love You."

He said to him, "Feed My lambs."

16 He said to him again a second time, "Simon, son of Jonah, do you love Me?"

He said to Him, "Yes, Lord; You know that I love You."

He said to him, "Tend My sheep."

17 He said to him the third time, "Simon, son of Jonah, do you [f]love Me?" Peter was grieved because He said to him the third time, "Do you love Me?"

And he said to Him, "Lord, You know all things; You know that I love You."
Jesus said to him, "Feed My sheep. 18 Most assuredly, I say to you, when you were younger, you girded yourself and walked where you wished; but when you are old, you will stretch out your hands, and another will gird you and carry you where you do not wish." 19 This He spoke, signifying by what death he would glorify God. And when He had spoken this, He said to him, "Follow Me."

Fun and Games

My cousin and I often sat on the porch and played the "My Car, Your Car" or "That's My Car" game. How it worked—We would decide who went first. The first car that drove by the front porch automatically belonged to the person who was first; therefore, if I were the first person, then the first car that went past automatically belonged to me, whether the car was a piece of junk or fancy. Then, the second car would belong to my cousin. This game would often generate a lot of laughter. The one who had the best cars at the end of the game would be declared the winner. Even though it was make-believe, it served as a motivator for our future because when we were kids, a nice car also symbolized success. By the way, if we became too loud, we were sometimes told to transition to the "Quiet Game." The "Quiet Game" is a children's game where children must stay quiet and not make a sound. The last child to make a noise wins the game. We would also play a game of checkers every now and then and not to mention, "Hide-and-Go-Seek". Hide-and-Go-Seek is a popular children's game in which at least two players (usually at least three) conceal themselves in the yard around the porch, to be found by one or more seekers. The game is played by one chosen player (designated as being "IT") counting to a predetermined number with eyes closed while the other players hide. After reaching this number, the player who is "IT" calls out, "Ready or not, here I come!" Then, he or she attempts to locate all concealed players. The porch served as the starting point before you found your hiding spot.

ECCLESIASTES 11:9   Rejoice, O young man, in your youth,
And let your heart cheer you in the days of your youth;

Walk in the ways of your heart,
And in the sight of your eyes;
But know that for all these
God will bring you into judgment.
10   Therefore remove sorrow from your heart,
And put away evil from your flesh,
For childhood and youth are vanity.

PROVERBS 15:13   A merry heart makes a cheerful countenance,
But by sorrow of the heart the spirit is broken.

PROVERBS 17:22   A merry heart does good, like medicine,
But a broken spirit dries the bones.

Land on your Feet

On the porch is where I learned the concept of "land on your feet." We used to throw the cat off the porch upside down; surprisingly, the cat would land on its feet. We would then slightly twist the cat and flip the cat off the porch in a tumbling motion, but the cat would somehow always land on its feet. To land on your feet is a common phrase that means to be in good condition or in a good situation after having a bad or difficult experience. It means to survive after a difficult and challenging situation. No matter how we threw the cat off the porch or the condition that the cat was in between the toss from the porch and the landing, the cat managed to adjust in midair and land on its feet. As I matured and navigated through life, I gained courage from the concept of the cat's tenacity—and through God's help, landed on my feet. No matter what you might be facing right now in life, through God's help, you can land on your feet. Like me, you may have stumbled a few times and even been knocked off your feet, but with Christ, you can regain your footing and land on your feet! PHILIPPIANS 4:13 states, "I can do all things through Christ who strengthens me."

Amazingly, sometimes the best thing that can happen to you is getting knocked off your feet. Moreover, sometimes it takes a traumatic event in life to cause us to look to the one who can enable us to land on our feet and move forward in life. Even as it happened to Saul in the Bible (whose name was changed to Paul—ACTS 13:9) on the road to Damascus:

ACTS 9:1 Then Saul, still breathing threats and murder against the disciples of the Lord, went to the high priest 2 and asked letters from him to the synagogues of Damascus, so that if he found any who were of the Way, whether men or women, he might bring them bound to Jerusalem 3 As he journeyed he came near Damascus, and suddenly a light shone around him from heaven. 4 Then he fell to the ground, and heard a voice saying to him, "Saul, Saul, why are you persecuting Me?" 5 And he said, "Who are You, Lord?" Then the Lord said, "I am Jesus, whom you are persecuting. It is hard for you to kick against the goads." 6 So he, trembling and astonished, said, "Lord, what do You want me to do?" Then the Lord said to him, "Arise and go into the city, and you will be told what you must do." 7 And the men who journeyed with him stood speechless, hearing a voice but seeing no one.

8 Then Saul arose from the ground, and when his eyes were opened he saw no one. But they led him by the hand and brought him into Damascus. 9 And he was three days without sight, and neither ate nor drank.

ACTS 26:12 "While thus occupied, as I journeyed to Damascus with authority and commission from the chief priests, 13 at midday, O king, along the road I saw a light from heaven, brighter than the sun, shining around me and those who journeyed with me. 14 And when we all had fallen to the ground, I heard a voice speaking to me and saying in the Hebrew language, 'Saul, Saul, why are you persecuting Me? It is hard for you to kick against the goads.' 15 So I said, 'Who are You, Lord?' And He said, 'I am Jesus, whom you are persecuting. 16 But rise and stand on your feet; for I have appeared to you for this purpose, to make you a minister and a witness both of the things which you have seen and of the things which I will yet reveal to you. 17 I will deliver you from the Jewish people, as well as from the Gentiles, to whom I now send you, 18 to open their eyes, in order to turn them from darkness to light, and from the power of Satan to God, that they may receive forgiveness of sins and an inheritance among those who are sanctified by faith in Me.'

Senior Leader Platform

During the family reunion at Grandma's house, the porch was a platform for senior leaders. The senior leaders and/or elderly relatives sat on the porch while everyone else took spots on the yard below the porch. The patriarchs and matriarchs of the family sat on the porch in a conversation that was only understood by many years of time and experience. They had seen what we had not, and like Dr. Martin Luther King Jr., they could tell you that they had seen the mountaintop and had a glimpse of the other side. Many things were spoken that we could not yet comprehend. One thing was for sure, our senior leaders had great faith and powerful testimonies of God's goodness. They urged and warned us, no matter how successful we would become, to never forget God. The senior leaders would also call the younger kids up on the porch whom they had not met to get to know them, or kids would simply want to ask questions from the elders of the family, which was a great opportunity for us to learn how we were all related. Plus, someone always brought a new boyfriend or girlfriend to the family reunion. Whomever the new person was in attendance had to definitely be ready for an interrogation from the senior leaders of the family. Those senior leaders weren't impressed by what you drove; they were more interested in what drove you. They would also observe and listen to the conversations to ensure that the standards of the family were kept and would call into question anyone who appeared to violate the standards during the family reunion. Ultimately, this was a joyful time to see everyone again. I always felt that it was a great privilege and blessing to be a part of our family, regardless of how you got there. On that porch, despite how successful you became, we were always reminded that our blessings came from God.

DEUTERONOMY 8:10 When you have eaten and are full, then you shall bless the Lord your God for the good land which He has given you.

11 "Beware that you do not forget the Lord your God by not keeping His commandments, His judgments, and His statutes which I command you today, 12 lest—when you have eaten and are full, and have built beautiful houses and dwell in them; 13 and when your herds and your flocks multiply, and your silver and your gold are multiplied, and all that you have is multiplied; 14 when your heart is lifted up, and you forget the Lord your God who brought you out of the land of Egypt, from the house of bondage; 15 who led you through that great and terrible wilderness, in which were fiery serpents and scorpions and thirsty land where there was no water; who brought water for you out of the flinty rock; 16 who fed you in the wilderness with manna, which your fathers did not know, that He might humble you and that He might test you, to do you good in the end— 17 then you say in your heart,

'My power and the might of my hand have gained me this wealth.'

18   "And you shall remember the Lord your God, for it is He who gives you power to get wealth, that He may establish His covenant which He swore to your fathers, as it is this day.   19   Then it shall be, if you by any means forget the Lord your God, and follow other gods, and serve them and worship them, I testify against you this day that you shall surely perish.   20   As the nations which the Lord destroys before you, so you shall perish, because you would not be obedient to the voice of the Lord your God.

Coming Off the Porch

If one of the parents, aunts, uncles, or grandparents had to come off the porch to discipline a disobedient or rebellious child, it could spell trouble and embarrassment for that child. That would not be a good day for us as children. There were times when the children would get a little rowdy, and the adults would only let it go so far. I use the phrase "come off the porch" today in business meetings. Before things get out of hand, don't just sit there, come off the porch. Curse words (we called "ugly words" back then), fighting, stealing, cheating, and lying would mean big trouble around the porch. Back in the day, disobedience as a child would result in a good old-fashioned spanking by hand on the buttocks or with a switch. What was more painful inwardly was when you were told to get your own switch. If it was too small, then the adults would get to choose the switch. Your best option was to do it right the first time, although painful, get the medium size switch, and get it over with. You may have gotten laughed at by the other children and cousins, but it worked two-fold because it put good fear in us and gave others a good example of what not to do. During those times, our parents and grandparents did not abuse us; they disciplined us. Many of us stayed out of jail, prison, and avoided premature death simply because somebody cared enough to come off the porch and prevented a doorway for evil to enter the family line.

PROVERBS 22:15   Foolishness is bound up in
     the heart of a child;
     The rod of correction will drive it far from
     him.

PROVERBS 23:13   Do not withhold correction
     from a child,

For if you beat him with a rod, he will not die. 14 You shall beat him with a rod, and deliver his soul from hell.

PROVERBS 19:18 Chasten thy son while there is hope, and let not thy soul spare for his crying.

PROVERBS 29:15 The rod and rebuke give wisdom,
But a child left to himself brings shame to his mother.

HEBREWS 12:5 And you have forgotten the exhortation which speaks to you as to sons: "My son, do not despise the chastening of the Lord,
Nor be discouraged when you are rebuked by Him;
6 For whom the Lord loves He chastens,
And scourges every son whom He receives."
7 If you endure chastening, God deals with you as with sons; for what son is there whom a father does not chasten? 8 But if you are without chastening, of which all have become partakers, then you are illegitimate

and not sons. 9 Furthermore, we have had human fathers who corrected us, and we paid them respect. Shall we not much more readily be in subjection to the Father of spirits and live? 10 For they indeed for a few days chastened us as seemed best to them, but He for our profit, that we may be partakers of His holiness. 11 Now no chastening seems to be joyful for the present, but painful; nevertheless, afterward it yields the peaceable fruit of righteousness to those who have been trained by it.

Today, things have changed due to the fact that some unlearned and unloving parents abuse their children, instead of providing discipline with love. Therefore, laws have been put in place to protect those children. On the other hand, disobedient and mischievous children have manipulated the law against their parents. Sadly, many of these children have shortened their lives.

EPHESIANS 6:1 Children, obey your parents in the Lord, for this is right. 2 "Honor your father and mother," which is the first commandment with promise: 3 "that it may be well with you and you may live long on the earth."

4   And you, fathers, do not provoke your children to wrath, but bring them up in the training and admonition of the Lord.

A Place of Counsel

Many times, counsel and advice were given on the porch. It was especially a place for warning about potential significant others, the do's and don'ts in relationships. We learned about the importance of no sex before marriage, and we were taught that the only safe sex was no sex before marriage. Often, the atmosphere on the porch was conducive for receiving counsel on various topics in an unthreatening environment. You didn't worry about eavesdropping because scenery from the porch took away the insecurity of the moment.

PROVERBS 11:14 Where no counsel is, the people fall: but in the multitude of counselors there is safety.

PROVERBS 15:22 Without counsel purposes are disappointed: but in the multitude of counselors they are established.

PROVERBS 24:3 Through wisdom a house is built,
And by understanding it is established;
4 By knowledge the rooms are filled
With all precious and pleasant riches.
5 A wise man is strong,
Yes, a man of knowledge increases strength;
6 For by wise counsel you will wage your own war,
And in a multitude of counselors there is safety.

GALATIANS 6:1 Brethren, if a man is overtaken in any trespass, you who are spiritual restore such a one in a spirit of gentleness, considering yourself lest you also be tempted.

A Place of Safety

On the porch, we could enjoy a soft rain and the cool refreshing air that it brought without getting wet. If I were caught in a storm without an umbrella, I just hopped onto the first available porch to wait out the storm. If I were locked out of my house, I could easily visit with a neighbor who would more than likely invite me to rest in a rocking chair on the porch and then hand me a glass of lemonade, sweet tea, or soda. It seemed like an unspoken truth that the front porch was the place where parents, older siblings, and neighbors could keep watch on every child in the community. Perhaps that same sensibility is true in some neighborhoods today. Although being raised in the country with a southern perspective, I've also lived in the city where there is more of a sense of privacy and security that always makes me think twice before setting foot uninvited on someone's porch. Children in the country had to be back on the porch before the streetlights came on. Not being on the porch by dawn could result in big trouble with your parents; being on the porch before the streetlights came on gave a sense of safety and security.

PSALMS 61:3   For You have been a shelter for me, a strong tower from the enemy.

JOHN 3:16   For God so loved the world that He gave His only begotten Son, that whoever believes in Him should not perish but have everlasting life. 17 For God did not send His Son into the world to condemn the world, but that the world through Him might be saved. 18 "He who believes in Him is not condemned; but he who does not believe is condemned already, because he has not believed in the name of the only begotten Son of God. 19 And this is the condemnation, that the light has come into the world, and men loved darkness rather than light, because their deeds were evil. 20 For everyone practicing evil hates the light and does not come to the light, lest his deeds should be exposed. 21 But he who does the truth comes to the light, that his deeds may be clearly seen, that they have been done in God."

A Place of Meditation

The porch provided a place to talk to God and a place where He could talk to you. I could take my journal, Bible, and/or iPad and tea or coffee to the porch very early in the morning to talk to God and hear the world coming to life for a new day. It's only when we slow down that we actually catch up to God. Meditation on God's Word and His plan for our lives does not only make us wise to salvation but guides us in our everyday life. My brothers, sister, cousins, and I might use the word *tranquility* to describe our memories of our time spent on our parents' and grandparents' porch.

JOSHUA 1:8 This Book of the Law shall not depart from your mouth, but you shall meditate in it day and night, that you may observe to do according to all that is written in it. For then you will make your way prosperous, and then you will have good success.

PROVERBS 3:5 Trust in the Lord with all your heart,
And lean not on your own understanding;
6 In all your ways acknowledge Him,
And He shall direct your paths.
7 Do not be wise in your own eyes;
Fear the Lord and depart from evil.

PSALM 1:1 Blessed is the man
Who walks not in the counsel of the ungodly,
Nor stands in the path of sinners,
Nor sits in the seat of the scornful;
2 But his delight is in the law of the Lord,
And in His law he meditates day and night.

1 TIMOTHY 4:11 Let no one despise your youth, but be an example to the believers in

word, in conduct, in love, in spirit, in faith, in purity. 13 Till I come, give attention to reading, to exhortation, to doctrine. 14 Do not neglect the gift that is in you, which was given to you by prophecy with the laying on of the hands of the eldership. 15 Meditate on these things; give yourself entirely to them, that your progress may be evident to all. 16 Take heed to yourself and to the doctrine. Continue in them, for in doing this you will save both yourself and those who hear you.

Relationship Building

Relationships were strengthened sitting on the porch. Family secrets and true feelings were shared sitting on the porch. One of the best places to get to know your significant other was sitting on the porch. You drew closer while sitting on the porch. Intimate conversations were shared on the porch. Sometimes the most unforgettable date was experienced sitting on the porch. Oftentimes, it was the determining factor of whether or not the person would be the one. Goals, desires, and concerns were shared on the porch. It's almost analogous to when God said to draw nigh to Him, and I will draw nigh to you.

JAMES 4:8 Draw near to God and He will draw near to you.

1 KINGS 7:1 But Solomon was building his own house thirteen years, and he finished all his house. 2 He built also the house of the forest of Lebanon; the length thereof was an hundred cubits, and the breadth thereof fifty cubits, and the height thereof thirty cubits, upon four rows of cedar pillars, with cedar beams upon the pillars. 3 And it was covered with cedar above upon the beams, that lay on forty five pillars, fifteen in a row. 4 And there were windows in three rows, and light was against light in three ranks.

5 And all the doors and posts were square, with the windows: and light was against light in three ranks. 6 And he made a porch of pillars; the length thereof was fifty cubits, and the breadth thereof thirty cubits: and the porch was before them: and the other pillars and the thick beam were before them.

7 Then he made a porch for the throne where he might judge, even the porch of

judgment: and it was covered with cedar from one side of the floor to the other. 8 And his house where he dwelt had another court within the porch, which was of the like work. Solomon made also an house for Pharaoh's daughter, whom he had taken to wife, like unto this porch. 9 All these were of costly stones, according to the measures of hewed stones, sawed with saws, within and without, even from the foundation unto the coping, and so on the outside toward the great court. 10 And the foundation was of costly stones, even great stones, stones of ten cubits, and stones of eight cubits. 11 And above were costly stones, after the measures of hewed stones, and cedars.

12 And the great court round about was with three rows of hewed stones, and a row of cedar beams, both for the inner court of the house of the Lord, and for the porch of the house.

Place of Memories

The porch held fond memories of good times lived in the past. It became a repository of experiences and milestones in our life. As I reminisce, I can visualize past generations of relatives who once sat on the porch. I see their faces, hear their voices, and see their clothing. Grandma's porch had a lot of memories that I will forever cherish. I remember all of the family reunions that took place centered around the porch, and the farther that I look back, the farther ahead I can see. As I reflect and celebrate the times on my grandmother's porch, respect and honor engender overwhelming gratitude. Reflection inspires respect, and reflection turns experience into insight. I am sure that there are so many stories about events on one's porch that are similar to mine. It's amazing how an architectural design of a porch can provide significant blessings to a home, family, and community.

Since the end of the nineteenth century, the American porch became a privileged background for family portraits. Sometimes I think about how many people must long for those front porch moments again- those moments when time stood still for a bit, and laughter passed through the air, many didactic and divine moments. Some of the best ways to treasure the small things and those memories are to capture them by photos and journaling.

Along life's journey, we can ponder on things now and understand better the lessons that we were taught along the way. That is why it's important to cherish the moments on your walk with Christ. You might not know exactly what He is doing, but you know that something is being done for our betterment.

LUKE 2:19   But Mary treasured up all these things, pondering them in her heart.

EPHESIANS 2:12   That at that time ye were without Christ, being aliens from the commonwealth of Israel, and strangers from the covenants of promise, having no hope, and without God in the world: 13   But now in Christ Jesus ye who sometimes were far off are made nigh by the blood of Christ.

1 CORINTHIANS 11:23   For I received from the Lord that which I also delivered to you: that the Lord Jesus on the same night in which He was betrayed took bread;   24   and when He had given thanks, He broke it and said, [a]"Take, eat; this is My body which is [b]broken for you; do this in remembrance of Me."   25   In the same manner He also took the cup after supper, saying, "This cup is the new covenant in My blood. This do, as often as you drink it, in remembrance of Me."   26   For as often as you eat this bread and drink this cup, you proclaim the Lord's death till He comes.

PSALM 77:11   "I will remember the works of the Lord;
Surely I will remember Your wonders of old.

12   I will also meditate on all Your work,
And talk of Your deeds.
13   Your way, O God, is in the sanctuary;
Who is so great a God as our God?
14   You are the God who does wonders;
You have declared Your strength among the
peoples.

PSALM 143:5   "I remember to think about the
many things you did in years gone by. Then
I lift my hands in prayer, because my soul is
a desert, thirsty for water from you.

HEBREWS 13:8   "Jesus Christ is the same
yesterday and today and forever."

PSALM 9:1   "I will give thanks to the Lord
with my whole heart; I will recount all of
your wonderful deeds."

JOHN 14:26   "But the Helper, the Holy Spirit,
whom the Father will send in my name, he
will teach you all things and bring to your
remembrance all that I have said to you."

The Importance of a Return to Porch Sitting

After my experiences on the porch, I believe that a house without a porch is incomplete. Your investments today help shape your tomorrow. We are blessed to experience the joy of porch sitting. Never underestimate the power of God revealed on a porch. A porch serves many times as a stress reliever and a place to relax and decompress. In the book of Acts, people came back to the porch for physical and spiritual healing and deliverance.

ACTS 5:12 And through the hands of the apostles many signs and wonders were done among the people. And they were all with one accord in Solomon's Porch. 13 Yet none of the rest dared join them, but the people esteemed them highly. 14 And believers were increasingly added to the Lord, multitudes of both men and women, 15 so that they brought the sick out into the streets and laid them on beds and couches, that at least the shadow of Peter passing by might fall on some of them. 16 Also a multitude gathered from the surrounding cities to Jerusalem, bringing sick people and those who were tormented by unclean spirits, and they were all healed.

Many of us need to return to the porch to regain humility, to get back in-tuned with God, and to get back in alignment with the Gospel that was once and for all delivered to the saints. After a mess-up or break-up, some need to return to the porch simply to understand that God loves them, there is family who still loves them, and life is not over. Some, like me, started from the porch. Lessons from the porch are what keep many of us grounded. Falling off the porch helped us to understand not to get too close to the edge. In life, we must ensure that we're not careless by getting too close to the edge. Returning to the porch every now and then helps you to remember those times, to stay grounded, and to take one day at a time.

In my own life, I had to realize this. Many people were telling me which way to go with my life and how to live and walk with Jesus. I was given theologies, books, and sermons. Yet, I had to take everything back to God's Word as a gage or standard for my life. Once I did, the Holy Spirit opened my eyes to see the truth because I went to where truth was found. As a result, I realized that I had to return to the porch and recollect those who really gave me the words of life and those whose audio matched their video. They were the ones who showed me who Jesus was all about—a relationship, not just religion. I had to sit on their porch and learn from them. I thank God for showing me this lesson.

Each of us has a person or people influencing our lives. Who is the person whom you need to sit down with on the porch and have a glass of tea or coffee and listen to? Who is really giving you the words of life? Are you willing to return to their porch? When you do, you will be able to learn how to live out the words of life and really live a life that is pleasing to God.

Thank you for spending this precious time with me on the porch. It was an honor to have you join the conversation. May God bless and keep you and your family.

ACTS 16:31 And they answered, "Believe in the Lord Jesus [as your personal Savior and entrust yourself to Him] and you will be saved, you and your household [if they also believe]." (AMP)

APPENDIX

Different Types of Porches

In existence since prehistoric times, the porch—which gets its name from the Greek word "portico," referring to the columned entry to a classical temple—has been a destination for both relaxation and meeting for many millennia. Over the centuries, the porch, or at least similar structures, have been referred to by many names, including veranda, piazza, portico and lanai.

However, it wasn't until the end of the 19th century that the porch as we know it was established in America both as a term and a structure. Of course, porches have come a long way since their ancient origins. In fact, the typical porch has been reimagined into a number of styles, satisfying a myriad of abodes. Since each type of porch has its own differences, I'm breaking down the basics below just for you:

COLONNADE   A porch with a series of columns set at regular intervals and usually supporting the base of a roof structure.

PORTICO   Reflective of its Grecian roots, is a small, covered area right in front of a home's entryway. More times than not, a portico is supported by columns.

RAIN PORCH   A porch that is an extension of your home and has enough room for a seating area. Generally, this style has a roof extension that lets rain water flow away.

BACK PORCH   A porch typically found in the back of the home. Think of it as a covered deck.

LANAIS   An enclosed porch. This porch might be all the rage in Hawaii, but they have plenty of global appeal. Unlike sunrooms, a lanai typically boasts a concrete floor and is situated on the ground right next to the home.

LOGGIA   A covered outdoor corridor. Commonly used as a fancy word for porch, loggias can be found on both the ground floor and upper levels.

SCREENED-IN PORCH   A porch with a screened closure, a screen porch can be enjoyed year-round. Some people even refer to this style as a sun porch, sun room, or Florida room.

WRAPAROUND PORCH   A porch which flanks at least two sides of a home.

VERANDA   A long, open structure on the outside of a building that has a roof.

PIAZZA   An open public area in a town or city (especially in Italy) that is usually surrounded by buildings; an arcaded and roofed gallery.

NOTE:

All scriptures used are of the New King James Version and King James Version, except where noted otherwise.

New King James Version (NKJV)
King James Version (KJV)
Amplified Version (AMP)